THE BLUE BOOK OF

SELF-PUBLISHING

A Reference Guide

by

S.D. ANDERSON, Ph.D.

Anderson, PhD, Sharon D.

Cape Cod Publishing

Cape Cod, MA 02632

Published in the U.S.A.

ISBN: 978-1097481163

"Nothing is impossible. The word itself says, 'I'm possible'."

~~ Audrey Hepburn

ACKNOWLEDGMENTS

A special thank you to the members of the

Cape Cod Writers' Studio.

I wrote it for them

Also

Thank you to my Angels and Guides who insisted
that I write it and "book" it.

They kept me up nights working on it by the light
of the silvery moon. (no pun intended)

Don't you just love 'em?

WELCOME TO THE BLUE BOOK OF SELF-PUBLISHING

INTRODUCTION

This book is divided into easy-to-reference sections so that you can refer back to them whenever you need to clarify a particular concept or need help with a sequence.

I always teach my students that today's reader is a *Reader On The Run*. One who doesn't have time to plow through a lot of words to get the help they need. They want it 'now' and in simple format. Because that is my own personal desire, I try to keep my books simple and to-the-point. Save the prose for my fiction novels and even those are not very "prosaic".

THE WRITING

The first part of the book is dedicated to the writing of your manuscript, which is all about you, your ideas, and your creation.

As the book progresses,

this guide will split into TWO sections – E-BOOK and PRINT BOOK.

This may seem strange to you, BUT the processes are a little different.

If your only idea at this time is to create a simple e-book, then this section will helpfully point out the steps to take to get you there.

However, if a print book or paperback is your objective, the section devoted to creating a print book is where you will find the information you need to publish that format.

FORMATTING YOUR BOOK

This part is all about the book. There are similar points you should have in place for both book processes:

YOUR BOOK BLURB   This is the information you will use to describe your book on the back cover (print) and on your page front on your Amazon page. (Both)

YOUR BIO AND PHOTO This usually appears on the (print) book back cover, and inside the book in both formats.

BISAC CODES OR CATEGORIES the BISAC codes or categories for all published books. BISAC stands for **Book Industry Standards And Communications**

BISAC Subject Codes List, is a standard used by many companies throughout the supply chain to categorize books based on topical content.

KEYWORDS

Keywords are ideas and topics that define what your content is about. In terms of SEO, they're the words and phrases that searchers enter into search engines, also called "search queries."

TITLE and SUB-TITLE (final for both books)

Do your research here, check out other books in your genre to see that your title is different and stands out.

FRONT COVER

I recommend CANVA.com for this part of the process. It is a free (so far) program and extremely easy to use if you have even the most basic knowledge of computers. Once you have finished the front cover and you decide to do a print book, this part is easily downloaded into KDP in a JPG file and creates the front of your book.

POINT TO REMEMBER! ☺

The Five built in marketing tools are in your book already.

1. Title

2. Cover

3. Book Blurb

4. Author Bio

5. First Chapter

PUBLISHING YOUR BOOK

This part of the book focuses on the actual publishing of your book – again, all about the book – and the complete process, from the downloading to the pricing and distribution.

MARKETING YOUR BOOK

This part of the book focuses on the READER...

Who ARE your readers?

Where do they 'hang out'?

Do they know who you are?

Are you a best-selling AUTHOR?

Or do you have a BEST SELLING BOOK?

These are the topics covered in this book and hopefully it will be

THE BLUE BOOK OF SELF-PUBLISHING IS YOUR "GO-TO" REFERENCE TO REACH FOR WHEN YOU NEED HELP PUBLISHING YOUR MANUSCRIPT.

Contents

ON WRITING

One of the reasons I suggest a writers group, in our case, a writers' studio, is most manuscripts are not ready to publish on a professional level. You have spent months, years, writing this story, you owe it to the story, to yourself, and to your readers to make certain it is the best offering that you know how to produce at this time.

Before I begin this section, perhaps you might like to use the FOOLSCAP METHOD which means using a piece of paper (foolscap from Olde English writing techniques) translated into modern language is a Legal size Pad of paper. (approximate 8 ½ X 14 - See my website for the PDF file of this technique). The theory here is, the outline of your entire book should fit on this paper.

Here is my outline set to music (ha ha)

PLOT

Let us begin with the PLOT... I started to use characters first, but they carry the story forward, so PLOT is the first idea. This is the 'bones' of your story, the legend or background. The original idea. The point you want to make, to entertain, educate or inspire your reader.

SUB-PLOTS

This is a second or third plot running through the book/story that pushes the story along, sometimes providing obstacles for both the Protagonist and Antagonist.

LOCATION

Where does your story take place? In the present? Is it in an historical novel? Or does it take place in another galaxy. (Sci-Fi) Your reader needs to know where he/she is as your story unfolds…

LOVE INTEREST

Most stories need a little love in it, even if it is between a boy and his dog, or a mother-child. Something to pull on the emotions of your reader. This includes a happy ending or one that ends but leaves the reader wanting more.

PROTAGONIST

Your lead character, the one that everything happens to… either internally or externally.

ANTAGONIST

The Antagonist is your villain, your Snidely Whiplash with the curly moustache who ties Nell Fenwick down on the train tracks because she couldn't pay the rent. Of course, she is rescued by Dudley Do-Right of the Mounties. (get the idea?)

SUPPORT CHARACTERS

These are the pals, buddies, best girlfriends who help the Protagonist or the Antagonist along the way.

TIME FRAME

When does the story take place? One day? One Week? One Year? It helps the reader to know how long this drama is going on and when it will end.

SELF-EDITING

This is the point where you read the entire manuscript and start your editing process. Make changes so that your story flows. Then hand it over to a professional editor.

LINE EDITING

A line editor reads each page checking punctuation, word usage, spelling (Don't rely on spell check for this) another pair of eyes looking at your manuscript is so much better. Hint: try not to use family members as they might feel put-upon or ill-used.

CONTENT EDITING

A Content Editor looks at your story/manuscript and reads it for any "holes" or discrepancies in your story, i.e.: a character description that doesn't match. (blue eyes instead of green), names of places or things, and so forth...A good content editor is priceless, and so is a line editor They add the polish and shine to your story.

BETA READERS

Choose these carefully because they are another priceless asset. Beta readers read your story for readability and a reader's point-of-view. Two or three Beta Readers are best. They will, if asked, give you a 'true review' and one that you can trust.

FINAL EDITS

When all of these edits are complete and you have made the changes to your manuscript, (the most difficult and boring part of the process) and all the changes are done, I recommend putting the whole thing aside in a final file and leaving it for a few days. During this resting period, you can work on your cover or some marketing plan you may have devised. Then go back and read it for the last and final time.

SAVING YOUR BOOK

I recommend the two-file system. If you have already opened up a file folder on your desktop, do a *save-as file final* copy in a Microsoft Word docx file and in a same extension final copy PDF file on your desktop or in your file. Try to keep it where you have easy access to your work because you will need it during the publishing process. For clarification, you may want to delete any earlier files so you don't get them mixed up.

Also, in that same folder, put your bio and picture and your blurb file, then you have them all in one place. It is important that you have a backup file of everything, too.

PDF File

You can change any file into a PDF file in your Microsoft Word program. Use the drop-down menu and find that option. Click on it to save your save-as file into a PDF.

A .DOCX FILE

Your Microsoft Word save file will most probably have already saved your file to that format. You can check it to make certain by clicking on your closed document and reading the extension.

POINT TO REMEMBER

Your book is complete and ready to be formatted into an E-BOOK or a PAPERBACK.

Yahoo!

FORMATTING

RESEARCH

The first step to formatting your book is the RESEARCH.

So many young authors jump into the fray without a clue. Research means going out to libraries or your own bookshelf to decide what you want your book to look like. What size do you picture your book, in 8 ½ x 11 or something smaller? Bring a tape measure or a ruler and measure the size of the books. Avoid the hard covers because you will be using the soft-cover paperback method. You can do a hard cover, but the price to produce is high.

Once you have decided the size, now go into Amazon Books, and start researching books in your genre. When you find one that fits, scroll down to their publishing information, and see where the book is listed, in what categories. This will give you a clue as to how and where you will or should list your book.

COMPETITION

1. Who is your competition? Did you find some books that are in your genre that are comparable? (not the same because if this is what you found, then make the appropriate changes to yours) Competition is healthy.

2. What are their categories? This will help you decide where to place your title in the BISAC listings.

3. What are their rankings? If you are on the Amazon site, you can see their rankings in the same section where their categories are listed. The Rankings give you a clue where this book sits in the sea of other books.

TITLE (Final Choice)

If you haven't already made that final choice for your title, do so now. I wait to this point. Because in your research, you may have found your same title. Here is your chance to make the changes, if any.

SUB-TITLE (Final)

Same explanation here. Make your sub-title give the potential reader a clue as to what your book is about, not the whole story, but a gentle clue!

YOUR AMAZON BOOKSHELF

If you have not set up your Amazon account, then now is the time to do so.

Here are those particulars again:

AMAZON - KDP

I send you to and through the Amazon process because it is easy and you can do a print book from there. KDP stands for Kindle Direct Publishing (E-book)

To set up your account in Amazon (so you can receive your royalties) here is the process:

Log into the KDP Site.

Go to the 'set up an account'.

Follow the prompts......

You will need some personal information:

1. Name. Address, phone number

2. E-mail address you will use to log in

3. A password (If you have an Amazon account you can use that.)

4. Your business EIN number or your social for tax purposes

5. EIN (Employee's Identification Number)

6. Sole Proprietor - Social Security Number

7. Bank account for royalty payments.

    a. Account Number

    b. Routing Number

This is for tax purposes. You will receive a 1099 in January of the following year.

This process should give you your own personal

BOOKSHELF.

Here is where you keep track of your book(s), your book sales, your royalties, and payments. If you scroll to the top of your bookshelf you will see

BOOKS, REPORTS, COMMUNITY, KDP SELECT

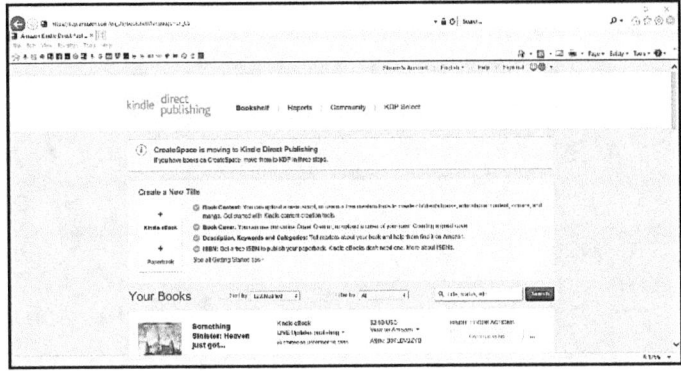

Figure 1

See the bar in this screen shot at the top of the screen?

POINT

Here is where we split into the two separate parts of your formatting.

E-BOOK FORMATTING

When you saved your Microsoft Word file in a docx. file keep it safe, because that is the file you will use to upload into KDP.

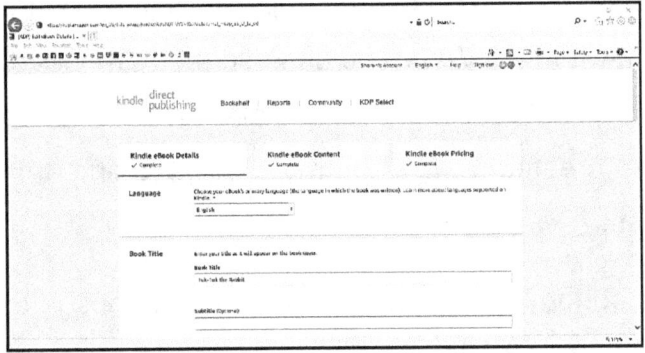

Figure 2

See the three headings across the top?

Kindle E-book details,

Kindle E-book content and

Kindle E-book Pricing.

Follow the prompts down the screen and you will set-up all the details – everything is self-explanatory... you have already done most of the work.

The same holds for your e-book content. This section is where you will download your docx. file and your cover.

The cover section is covered separately, if you want to work with CANVA or you can use the KDP Cover Creator. That's a simple feature already built-in and I have created a few of my covers using this process.

At the bottom of this screen you have the option to Preview Your Book.

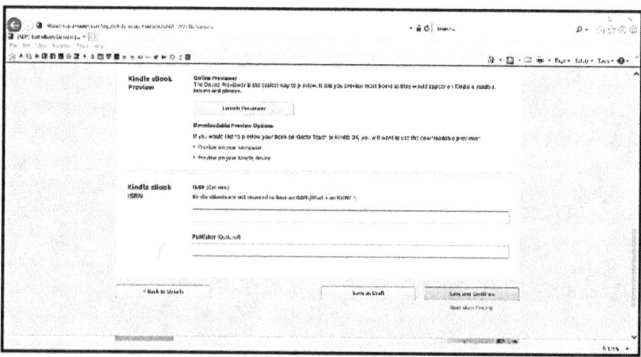

Figure 3

Take the time to PREVIEW your book. It will save you from possible embarrassment if you have not checked the preview thoroughly.

Once you are satisfied with what you see in the preview, follow the screens, and move forward into the next section.

PRICING

A word about pricing your book. When you did your research, you may have noted the pricing on those books similar to yours. Use your own judgment. It is very easy to think that your book is worth $9.99 but is that realistic? This section is similar to selling your house. You want a million trillion dollars for it because --- whatever reason, but the other houses on the market are only being offered for thousands. Which will sell? I know you understand this concept. Also consider that some of the books offered are by a traditional publisher with best-selling authors.

PUBLISH YOUR BOOK

This link is at the bottom of the Pricing Screen and having followed all the steps and you are satisfied, then go ahead and PUBLISH...

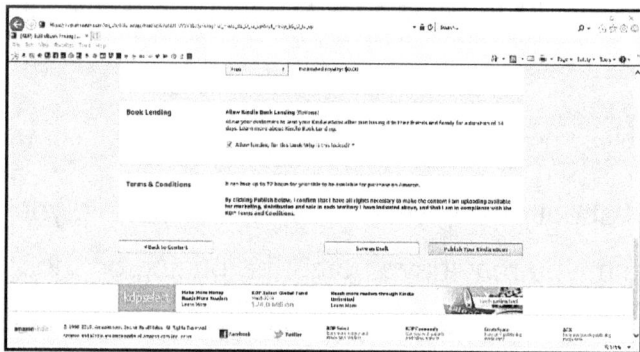

Figure 4

.

YAHOO!!!

Your E-book will be offered for sale in the following countries:

US

UK

DE

ES

FR

IT

NL

JP

BR

CA

MX

AU

Can you guess the countries from those letters?

United States, United Kingdom, Denmark, Spain, France, Italy, Netherlands, Japan, Brazil, Canada, Mexico, and Australia.

FORMATTING FOR PRINT

In your Microsoft Word file, open your final docx. file and do a save-as file naming it my book for print or whatever name you want to give it.

Open that file, checking to be certain it is your new file for print.

Click on LAYOUT at the top of your screen. You will have choices. Choose SIZE and click on that. Scroll down to MORE PAPER SIZES.

In that box you enter the size of the book you chose. (6 x 9) is the default size for a paperback in KDP. When you have entered the PAPER SIZE (6 X 9) the screen will automatically change the size of your manuscript to that book size.

Now go to the top of that small screen and click on MARGINS. Set them as follows:

Top, bottom and inside – 0.75"

Outside – 0.5"

Gutter – 0.13""

Mirror Margins

Section Start – New Page

Different odd and even

Different first page

Header – 0.4"

Footer – 0.3"

Those are the settings for your default 6 x 9 book.

Save and close and your book is automatically formatted to book size.

For additional directions on how to do this, I recommend my book *CREATING A PAPERBACK IN KDP*

https://www.amazon.com/dp/B0746NJ8PB   E-Book

https://www.amazon.com/dp/1548736740   Print edition

I wrote it to take you through step-by-step.

Using that new size, same file, here is the setup for the book.

TITLE PAGE

COPYRIGHT PAGE

You can use this one if you like:

© 2019 by Your Name

Your name, last, first middle initial

Book Title:

Book Summary:

ISBN 978- (KDP gives you one)

Name of your publishing company (optional)

Address: (optional)

Published in the U. S. A.

After the copyright page, insert a blank page,

Dedication Page

Blank Page

T.O.C. (Table of contents) optional

Acknowledgement Page

Blank Page

First chapter.

If your sequencing is correct, your first chapter should be on an odd numbered page.

Adding page numbers is easy. Go up to your ribbon at the top of your page, open INSERT and scroll along until you find PAGE NUMBERS. Click on that option and select the style you want to use in your book. Remember to close the Header/Footer and VOILA! you have page numbers.

POINT

Your FIRST CHAPTER should always begin on an odd numbered page. If you don't believe me, go to your library or one of your own books and open to the first chapter.

ILLUSTRATIONS

This might be a good place to suggest adding something on your chapter pages if you want. It all comes under the heading of formatting the interior of your book. In some of my books (the Something Series) I use FREE CLIP ART.

CHAPTER HEADINGS

You may use any type of font for your chapter headings, always remember to be consistent through the entire book.

FONT

The font you choose for your book is important. It relates the style of your story. You may also want to choose a READABLE font and one that clearly translates in both print and digital (e-book). This book is done in Arial 12 point. Do be choosy.

PARAGRAPHING

This can be done through the entire book without too much fuss. On your ribbon, go to paragraphs and click the arrow in the corner. You will get a screen that will allow you to set all of the spacing including line spacing for the entire book.

This may change some of your previous settings, but if you scroll through the complete book before you save it for a final save, you can line all of that up perfectly.

Remember to make two files of the finished completely-edited manuscript. One .docx and one PDF.

For a print book you will use the PDF file. The other is your backup.

ARE YOU READY TO MOVE ON?

On your KDP Bookshelf, click on the prompt for Creating Your Paperback.

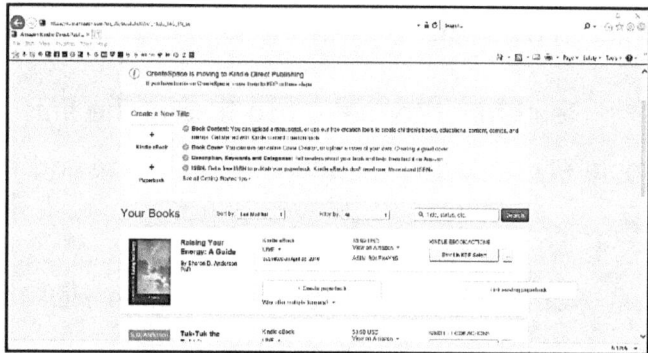

Figure 5

Fortunately, your e-book can be easily translated into a print book. You will get a screen asking you if you wish to do that. All of your data will be transferred over for your print version, even your cover. You will still need to download your PDF version of your print book.

PUBLISHING

Before we go much further, here is a glossary of terms you should be familiar with:

GLOSSARY OF TERMS

K.D.P. – Kindle Direct Publishing - An Amazon company for authors and publishers to publish their e-books worldwide for free, to be read electronically on Kindle, e-readers and other electronic devices. (tablets, computers, cell phones, etc.)

DASHBOARD - A software-based control panel for one or more applications, and for network devices. Your dashboard enables you to monitor and maintain your publications, in this instance, e-books and print books created on KDP or CreateSpace.

FORMAT - the way in which information is arranged or presented, especially in computers. A defined structure for the processing, storage or display of data. In books, the way the interior of the book is set up and presented for the reader.

TEMPLATE – a pre-set format of a document or file to be used so that the actual format does not have to be re-created each time it is to be used.

FRONT MATTER – the first section of the book in which the title, copyright, dedication, acknowledgements, preface, foreword, table of contents, and any other additional information pertinent to the book's interior is presented for the reader.

BACK MATTER- Just as front matter is what you find at the beginning of a book, back matter, simply put, is what you find at the end of a book—the sections that appear after the central story has been completed. These sections of back matter are often supplementary in nature, and inform the reader about some aspect of the book, or author.

META DATA - a set of data that describes and gives information about other data.

COPYRIGHT - the exclusive legal right, given to an originator or an assignee to print, publish, perform, film, or record literary, artistic, or musical material, and to authorize others to do the same.

BOOK INTERIOR - The inside pages of the book where your manuscript is placed for reading. In publishing programs, there are choices as to paper color, ink color (usually black) and interior with illustrations either in color or in black and white. The most common choices are:

Black ink on crème paper,

Black ink on white paper and

Color interior on white paper.

TRIM SIZE- The final size of a printed page after excess edges have been cut off is the trim size. Commercial printing companies often print several copies of one document on the same large sheet of paper.

BLEED SETTINGS - Bleed is a printing term that is used to describe a document which has images or elements that touch the edge of the page, extending beyond the trim edge and leaving no white margin. When a document has bleed, it must be printed on a larger sheet of paper and then trimmed down.

PAPERBACK - A paperback is a type of book characterized by a thick paper or paperboard cover, and often held together with glue rather than stitches or staples. In contrast, hardcover or hardback books are bound with cardboard covered with cloth. WIKIPEDIA

COVER FINISH – Paperback books offer two cover finishes in this program, GLOSS and MATTE. The gloss finish is shiny and has a sleek look. The matte cover is more subdued with a non-shiny finish and a pebbly feel. My preference is the matte finish.

SAVING YOUR FILES

We have done this one to death, but, remember the two file system and you won't lose anything. If you should inadvertently delete something, remember it is still on your computer – yes, in your recycle bin…

CHOOSING KEYWORDS

We have already referred to this one. If you Google the word 'keywords' and do some research, you should be able to come up with seven that will match your story. Most times they are already imbedded in your blurb or should be.

Figure 6

CHOOSING CATEGORIES

Already covered under BISAC or categories in the introduction. Book Industry Standards And Communications.

CHOOSING YOUR GENRE

This sounds easier than it really is. It took me three books before I found the genre to fit my stories.

66

Written Word Media has excellent descriptions for genres. I would suggest going there first.

ISBN

Your International Standard Book Number. Every print book has to have one. KDP will give you one of theirs for your book. It will read, Independently Published. If you plan on self-publishing a lot of books, you can purchase your own from BOWKER, the industry standard for ISBN numbers,

COPYRIGHT

The minute you place the symbol © on your book with your name, you have a copyrighted document or book. Feel free to use the suggestion earlier or go to one of your favorite books and see what their copyright information says.

WRITING YOUR BIO

Your bio or biography should be short and sweet. A two-page description of your life since the third grade is not necessary. All of your accolades and other laudatory entries can be saved for your website or some other location. The reader wants to know who you are, not what you have done.

YOUR BIO PICTURE

Noteworthy, your picture should be current and up-to-date. It is optional but does add to your character of who you are. Readers want to know what you look like. It is common curiosity.

OTHER BOOKS BY YOU

Again, the reader wants to know what else you have written. If this is your first book, and you have another started you can list that with a brief history and you could add a publishing year or just say *it's in process.*

YOUR BOOK BLURB

This is what will appear on the back panel of your book in print and in your description on Amazon KDP. Write it ahead of time so that you are prepared for this step. Suggestion? Keep it short and simple. Give the reader a glimpse of what your book is about and why they should read it.

CREATING YOUR COVER

I suggest this be done in two parts. If you like the cover you have created for your e-book, then use that for the front of your paperback. It keeps the identity together. From here you work in Cover Creator on your KDP site or dashboard.

CANVA

An easy to use FREE site (so far). They do have an Office Edition which you can subscribe to if you plan to do a great deal of graphic work. For the casual user, the FREE edition would be sufficient. On this screen shot, you can see the cover of my book, *Body Blogs*, completed on CANVA.

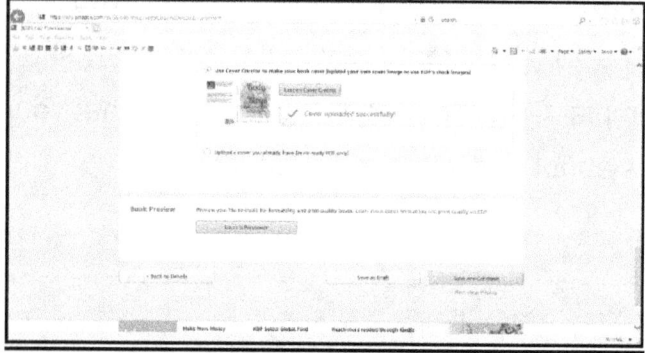

Figure 7

This is also the screen where you actually publish your book after approving your on-line proof and a physical "proof" of you book. If you are new to the process, a physical proof will help you see what changes, if any, you need to make before actually publishing. I have done more than one proof of a book to be certain it is "perfect".

POINT:

No one's book is ever perfect. You no sooner publish when you see or think of what you "should have done differently". Trust me, it happens to everyone. That is why being a self-publisher allows for any changes you might wish to make after publication. Traditional publishing is not that lenient.

UPLOADING YOUR FILES

Uploading your cover to KDP will be in a PDF file. A good practice for saving your file on CANVA when you download it to your computer is as a JPEG file because you may want to use it again in a blog or on your website. JPEG is a smaller file and usually accepted on most sites.

A WORD HERE ABOUT FILE EXTENSIONS:

PDF – is an acronym for PORTABLE DOCUMENT FORMAT.

JPEG- is a file extension for graphic files. It is an acronym for JOINT PHOTOGRAPHIC EXPERTS GROUP. This format is used throughout the industry. Also expressed as **JPG**.

PNG – is an acronym for PORTABLE NETWORK GRAPHICS.

GIF – is another acronym for GRAPHIC INTERCHANGE FORMAT.

As we progress in technology, more of these acronyms crop up into our language usage and eventually become as common to us as Smith.

PREVIEWING YOUR BOOK

An absolute must and not to be avoided. If you miss this step, your book may not be up to your high standards. There are two ways to do this previewing. Even the term says it is a PRE-VIEWING.

DIGITAL PREVIEW

KDP encourages you to view your book, cover and all, in an on-line previewer. For your e-book, your previewer is usually on a Kindle Fire or something similar. Your print book is offered for viewing in an on-screen previewer with the ability to turn the pages back and forth. This format is similar to your actual book.

ORDERING YOUR PROOF

Most writers and authors-to-be prefer to hold their book in hand. It does appear different in print and gives you the actual, see, feel, smell, of what your book will actually look like.

APPROVING YOUR PROOF

KDP does not allow you to skip over this step. It is Highly Recommended that you read your entire book three times. The first time for appearance and pagination, etc. The second for content, do the facts match up, etc. And the third for any grammatical errors. Here is where your Beta Readers are helpful.

Once you approve your proof, (see bottom of the page in this screen shot)

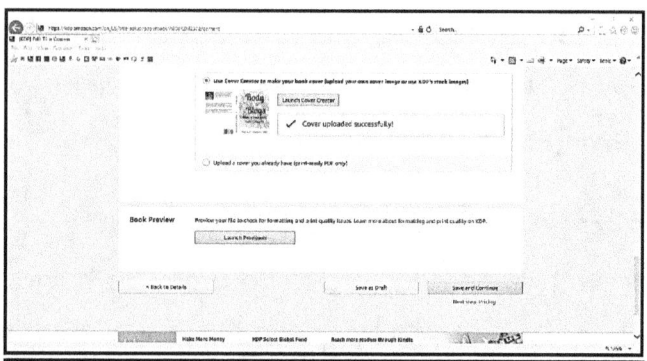

Figure 8

PRICING

Once you have approved your proof, you move on to the next screen, Pricing and Distribution.

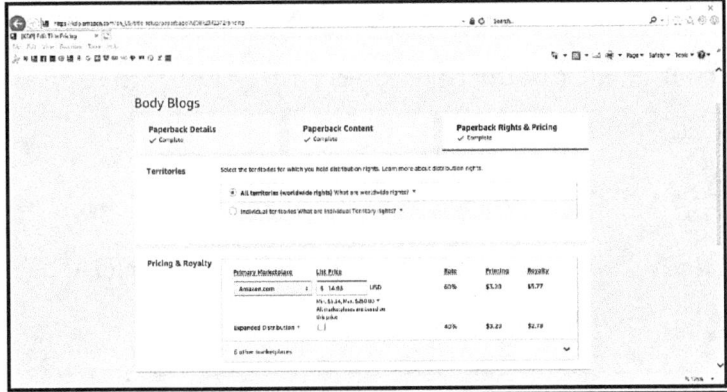

Figure 9

Depending on the page count of your book and the book size you have chosen, your pricing for a paperback should be within the range of other paperbacks out on the market. Remember, you want your book to sell, so check other books and see where they are priced.

Your pricing in other marketplaces (I believe there are six) will be determined by KDP for the currency exchange based on your book price.

EXTENDED DISTRIBUTION

This is an option KDP offers for you to have your book listed in BISAC.

BISAC

BISAC stands for BOOK INDUSTRY STANDARDS AND COMMUNICATIONS.

BISAC CODES

Are listings industry wide that are subject descriptors or categories where you list your book when you publish. The entire list is available on-line.

EXCLUSIVITY OR NOT (AMAZON OR?)

Here you decide if you want to publish exclusively with Amazon or use other sites. I recommend a few in the marketing segment of the book.

When you choose to publish exclusively with Amazon, you enroll your book in KDP SELECT which gives Amazon the right to have your book on their site EXCLUSIVELY for ninety days and if you select the auto-renewal box, your book stays with Amazon until you release it from that Select Group. You may have to wait out the tenure of that exclusivity to move your book elsewhere.

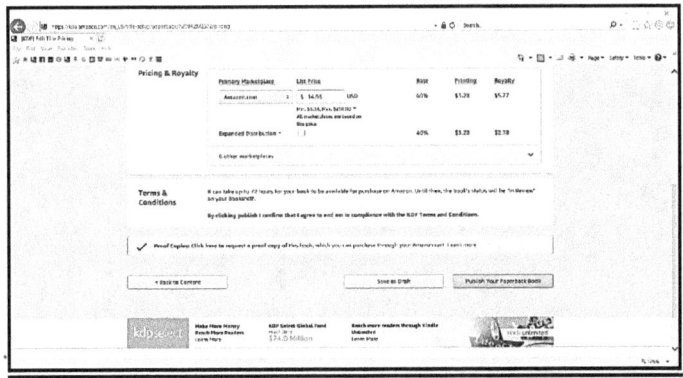

Figure 10

This screen shot is the last and final one for you. The Yellow bar is the one where you PUBLISH YOUR BOOK!

YAHOO!

MARKETING

HOW DO YOU WANT TO MARKET?

You have a few choices on the method you choose to market your book. There are three ways to aim your marketing efforts.

Is the focus on the book, itself?

Is the focus on you as the author?

Or is it both? That is a bit more difficult.

A BEST-SELLING BOOK

If you decide you want to have a "Best Selling Book", you feel your book is very important and will benefit humankind in some way, then that will be how you should aim your marketing efforts. Your BOOK becomes the focus of your marketing and the story it tells. You can also talk about your characters and how they deal with the conflicts in the book. You may decide to use the BOOK to make a statement, or the benefits the reader will gain by reading your BOOK. I think you get that point.

A BEST-SELLING AUTHOR

Here your marketing tactics change and the focus points to you, the Best Selling Author because ... you are an expert in this field of writing. You have ninety-nine other books you have published on your shelf and this is ---(you fill in the blanks here). You are the focus. The book is a by-product of your other books, or you have discovered an innovative something that will make life easier if you read the remarkable breakthrough – yaddah, yaddah, yaddah.. I know you got that one!

LOCAL OR GLOBAL?

More choices.

I have witnessed a few new authors doing the local scene. They go from bookstore to bookstore in and around their town or city and setup book signings or book talks. They sell perhaps forty to sixty books which includes family and friends. This is a delightful way to market your book. You get to meet your readers first-hand and speak with them directly. This is an excellent way to market your books, and a very arduous way. It is your first step in building your "Platform". When you tie it in with social media, you have the next step in selling your book(s) globally.

INTERNET MARKETING

I am such an advocate of using the Internet to sell books because I am an introvert (as most writers are) and am petrified to leave my computer, pajamas, and bunny slippers at home. Local bookstores would frown on that.

Internet marketing is becoming 'the thing'. More and more authors are paying for ads to sell their book and becoming quite successful. Amazon has been offering this option for over a year and I have noticed our book pages have several tiers of ads from "*Those who purchased, also purchased...*" and many other spotlights.

WHO ARE YOUR READERS?

Before you run out and start spending $$$ on ads, find out who your readers really are. Are they "READERS ON THE RUN"? Will they be happy with an e—book? E-book sales will triple over the next year so consider using this tactic to promote your book.

GENRE

It is important that you know what genre you are writing in and to, because that is where your readers are hiding. Well, their e-mail addresses are hiding.

SUBSCRIBERS

Are people who have subscribed to a service to receive notifications that there are books in their genre available at a discount or are being offered for free.

SOCIAL MEDIA

You already know who they are. Facebook, Twitter, Pinterest, Instagram, and many more are there for your discovery and use. They each have their own set of rules, so check carefully before you dive in.

ON-LINE SOURCES

I will touch on this here. My work has been exploring these three on-line marketing services. You can sign up for free and explore what they have to offer. These are the ones I have found to be the most practical to use as far as ease and expense. There are more on the internet and you might find them to your liking. My foray into this area of marketing have given me good results and I keep using them because they work.

WRITTEN WORD MEDIA

I only have good things to say about this site. They are trustworthy in giving what they offer, and stand behind their service. One of my students ran a promotion and was dissatisfied. Her money was immediately refunded. They also offer sound information about the industry and have made some very excellent predictions.

I recommend using their definitions on genres if you are uncertain what genre you are writing in.

BOOKBUB

This service has been around for a few years and are easy to use. My take on them is they are similar to Goodreads only much better. Their pricing range for ads is more expensive than Written Word Media, but they are also reputable.

DRAFT2DIGITAL

A favorite of mine. I like to think of D2D as my agent. When I list any of my books with them, they send it out to eleven different services. It would take me days to do that and months to follow-up. I would never have any time to write, let alone keep track of what was happening and where my royalties were coming from. They do take a very small percentage of your royalties, but the exposure is well worth it.

LONG-TERM CAREER OR INSTANT FAME

This is a question you need to ask yourself consistently. Why am I writing and what do I want to happen? Do I want a quick claim-to-fame or do I want a career for the next twenty years or more?

Books are SCALABLE INCOME. One book will keep selling for years and you only had to write it once. The choice is yours to make.

This section concludes the first part of the book. The next part is more prosaic.

Happy Reading.

Part Two

The prosaic part

Two questions writers frequently ask about their manuscript:

1. What should I do with it?

2. How do I do it?

To answer your first question, you have two options: You can try to have it published by the traditional route – which means writing query letters and sending them out to a lot of publishing houses and/or agents, OR you can self-publish your manuscript. That is what this part of the book and I am all about.

The answer to the second question is: there are ways to accomplish this but it depends on how much you are willing to do, and how many computer skills you have. Anyone can self-publish a book.

A good definition for self-publishing is:

*"**Self-publishing** is the publication of any book, album or other media by its author without the involvement of an established publisher. Unlike the traditional publishing model in which control of the*

publication is shared with a publisher, the author controls the entire process in a self-publishing effort including the design of the cover and the interior, price, distribution, marketing, and public relations. The authors can do all of these activities by themselves or they may outsource these tasks."

Source – Wikipedia

Also, from Wikipedia, came this side bar of interesting predictions from a website new to me but a nice resource:

www.writtenwordmedia.com

And this quote:

"For decades, the literary world dismissed self-published authors as amateurs and hacks who lacked the talent to land a book deal. But that attitude gradually began to change with the rise of e-books and the arrival of Kindle from Amazon, *which gave authors direct access to millions of readers."*

— Alexandra Alter in the New York Times, 2016

An excellent summary of the self-publishing world over the last 20 years…

Self-Publishing isn't easy, it takes demanding work and dedication, as my students will tell you now that they are well into the task.

One of the questions you should ask yourself is:

What are my expectations after I publish my book?

Self-Publishing is not a "get-rich-quick scheme", although there are many authors who will sell you their book proclaiming that if you follow what they tell you, you will.

Yes, you'll sell copies of your book to friends and relations, and a few at the local bookstore. If you do a book signing, you will sell some there. Then what?

Is your focus just on the writing and become a famous author? Or do you want a career in writing?

My focus is on using my writing to help other writers achieve their publishing dreams, by building a business of how-to books, audio books, and have my own career as an author.

Think about what YOU really want to create as a self-publisher.

Here is a summary of the Self-Publishing Process for a paperback book:

1. Idea and concept

2. Writing the story outline

3. Rewriting

4. Story editing for plot, etc.

5. More rewriting to polish the manuscript

6. Copy editing for semi-final copy

7. Copy out to Beta Readers (4 or 5)

8. Make any changes for final copy

9. Layout and formatting

10. Cover design

11. ISBN purchase (optional)

12. Select categories and keywords

13. Pricing

14. Distribution channels

15. Upload documents

16. Preview

17. Make changes (if any)

18. Resubmit edited copy and/or cover

19. Order proofs

20. Receive proofs and accept or make further changes

21. Order Author copies

22. Marketing and promotion

Here is the process for an e-book, not as involved, but still necessary.

1. Idea and concept

2. Writing the story outline

3. Rewriting

4. Story editing for plot, etc.

5. More rewriting to polish the manuscript

6. Copy editing for semi-final copy

7. Copy out to Beta Readers (4 or 5)

8. Make any changes for final copy

9. Cover design

10. Select categories and keywords

11. Pricing

12. Distribution channels

13. Upload documents (cover and text)

14. Preview

15. Make changes (if any)

16. Resubmit edited copy and/or cover

17. Preview book

18. Marketing and promotion

Are you discouraged? Don't be. If you work through the process step-by-step you will end up with a terrific book. Who knows, it may be a best seller.

What you are reading is the most up-to-date information on self-publishing that I have to date.

The actual art of self-publishing has not changed, the basic concepts still are the same, what has changed is the attitude towards self-publishers and the tools available to carry out those goals.

Back in 'them-thar-days', self-publishers were considered self-absorbed, egotistical vanity authors who were not worthy to be considered by a traditional publishing house. Their only choice was to pay thousands of dollars to have their well-written and worthy manuscript in print.

Then, along came Amazon in 2008 and changed everything. They introduced a new way to read books. They introduced the e-book.

Times have changed drastically since I began self-publishing in 1998. Then it was the church bulletin and a directory of restaurants. Now, with Amazon and the global connection through the world wide web, anything is possible.

Amazing there are still some who feel that to self-publish is not proper, or worse, not worthy. (did you get that Bostonian accent in there?)

Where I live, we still have a few local libraries and traditional book stores that WILL NOT ACCEPT a self-published book, even though it took years to write, edit, edit again, re-write, and edit one more time so that it would be fit for human consumption.

(Warning! This is my soap-box, FYI.)

We are in the digital age, are we not? And every cell phone, iPhone, Android, Kindle, Nook, tablet, laptop, and computer have a reader attached, sometimes more than one.

Would You People Please Wake Up and Smell the Intel Chips???

Allow me to repeat this:

We are in the digital age, are we not? And every cell phone, iPhone, Android, Kindle, Nook, Tablet, Laptop, and Desk Top Computer have a reader attached, sometimes more than one.

Sorry, it just came out!

How many of you has a stack of rejection letters from traditional publishers somewhere in your closet? I used mine to wallpaper the bathroom as a reminder to never think along traditional publishing lines again.

Self-publishing does not carry the stigma it used to. Especially now that some self-published authors are making a six-figure income from their self-publishing sites, and many have given up their day job to become full-time writers/authors.

I won't bore you anymore with the TRADITIONAL vs SELF-PUBLISHING lore, I am certain you have heard it all, but if you haven't already thought about becoming a self-published author, please consider the idea as you go along in this book. I will devote a whole section to all the benefits of self-publishing.

You must be interested in self-publishing, otherwise you wouldn't be reading or listening to this book. It will be offered in both formats. (yes, another benefit of self-publishing.)

This BLUE BOOK is exactly that, a blue book or guide (like the ones they use for cars) to help you create your own self-publishing business. Or simply self-publish a single manuscript if you are not quite ready to go the complete Entrepreneur route.

I encourage you to read this Little Blue Book carefully, page-by-page, section-by-section, and familiarize yourself with the self-publishing world. If you ordered a print version, keep it handy as a reference like car salesmen do with the little blue book of cars.

I've covered most of what I know to date. This is a complete overview of the system I used to self-publish thirty-six books on Amazon, coach other writers to publish their work, and teach classes in self-publishing.

I truly believe if you follow this little Blue Book, you can easily create an e-book and a paperback book, (even an audio book) and publish it on Amazon. This could be the beginning of your own self-publishing career, and a six-figure income.

In the very near future, I expect to receive an email from you telling me how this Blue Book has changed your life, and you are now a successful self-publisher. Here's the address:

sdanderson.books@gmail.com

Although this book can be read as pure text, it is best to read it on a tablet or computer to click through the links for extra material.

If you find it useful, please share it with anyone else who might be interested in this information.

You have my permission to embed it on your blog, share it with your writers' group, on a forum or anywhere you like, email it to a friend or use excerpts on your site, providing you cite the source and don't sell the content.

Thank you,

The Audacious Publisher

a/k/a

Sharon D. Anderson

How I became a self-published author.

Not unlike your own story, I had been publishing church bulletins, then a dining directory (because I was new to the area and had no clue where the delicious food was). In this process, I learned to use several self-publishing programs. I also did a lot of other ventures, too. I won't bore you with those details. After wading through a pile of unsuccessful attempts in other endeavors, I decided to write my own book. I had my doctorate in the field of metaphysics, which was my then current field of expertise, but was still fascinated with the writing and publishing aspects of the computer age. I was hooked.

I had been doing a lot of research on writing and read somewhere in a book this tiny bit of advice: *'write about what you know.'*

Well, that was easy. I knew all about Angels and the Angelic Realm, so that is what I wrote about. At that time, no publishing house was interested in books about angels. The rejection slips were piling up and I was getting frustrated. (I still write about them, my Something Series; *Something Sinister, Something Bloody and Something Loverly*)

I was finally directed to BookLocker.com, who accepted my manuscript and I had my first book. *Angels in Action*.

I published four more books with them. This process was considered 'self-publishing', and although inexpensive as far as the industry of publishing houses, it was still costly.

My lifestyle changed, (I retired at that age of 65 and so did my income.) In 2009, I discovered KDP, a new subsidiary of Amazon who was making great strides in digital publishing, introducing the Kindle

Reader, (Kindle Direct Publishing) and I have been with them ever since.

I recommend Amazon and start my students to work with them because the process is easy and your book goes into print or digital quickly.

Amazon is the perfect venue for a newbie to begin their career in self-publishing, especially when you are just starting out and have limited income to invest.

In 2016, I founded the Cape Cod Writers Studio to help other writers learn how to publish their books on Amazon. We meet weekly at two local libraries (Dennis Public Library and Centerville Public Library) to polish our manuscripts and eventually publish them. The Dennis Studio has been open for over two years and four students have self-published, with two more in process. See my website for their success stories:

www.audacious-publisher.com

Self-Publishing as a business, not a hobby.

When you publish your first book, either e-book or print, you have created INVENTORY. Yup, you now have a product to sell. You are 'in business' as my parents used to say.

To be 'in business', you need a market place, somewhere to sell your inventory. You already have one and are using it now. Yes, the WWW or world wide web. This is your market place. Eventually, you will need to set up a 'storefront' in which to sell your books (Your website).

If you are familiar with social media and Facebook, you can create a Facebook business page and use that as a storefront, but a web address is preferable. That www.yourbook.com is part of your branding, your identity.

When you publish on Amazon, they give you a limited storefront (your landing page) and offer your book(s) globally in thirteen countries. Plus, they even convert your royalties from the different currencies into USD and deposit it into your own bank account. (not a bad deal, right?)

Yes, Amazon does take a small percentage of your royalties, but look at what they give back. You can claim a 70% or 35% royalty on e-books, your choice. Amazon does a lot of your marketing for you already. We will cover that later.

Much more of this is covered in my book: *Writing as a Retail Business*

Here is that link:

https://www.amazon.com/Writing-as-Retail-Business-Guide/dp/1530134625/

Writing – the WEEI method.

W – Writing to

E – Entertain

E – Educate

I – Inspire

As a Self-Publisher, it is your Duty? Moral Obligation? Whatever word you choose to use, it is that integrity that is needed to WEEI your readers – in other words – QUALITY WRITING.

You know exactly what I mean, so I won't elaborate further. When you write, place your reader in front of you, and tell him/her the story.

Programs for Writing

Which program is the best one for writing?

I usually recommend Microsoft Word. There are tons of writing programs, but the one most easily recognized, and easier to work with is Word. If you are working with another program, then I suggest that you switch your files over to this one for it will give you fewer headaches in the future if you are serious about continuing to self-publish.

I also have Scrivener on my computer, an excellent program to write in, but not easy to format. In fact, to format into book size, you really need the Word version.

Word is very powerful and will give you many options, especially if you intend to include small illustrations at the beginning of your chapters.

I have worked with several writers who were using other programs and formatting it into book size and dressing it up was a challenge.

MAC vs. PC

Depending what device, either a Mac or a PC, lap-top or desk-top, the writing should be done on the same program as recommended above: Microsoft Word.

I have always worked on a P.C. until I started training other writers in publishing when I discovered the difference. So, to MAC users, use whatever writing program you have and leave the formatting to Amazon for e-books. As for print books, to establish your size for your book, you may want to consider the default paperback size as a 6 x 9 and use your A5 paper size. Because, for a print book, you send it to publish in a PDF format, the formatting stays static or the same as you intended.

On your e-book, I recommend using KDP's Kindle Create program, a free download, that will help you with the set-up.

Self-Editing and Professional Editing

Editing is mandatory for both your e-book and/or your print book.

I cannot stress how very important editing is if you want to produce a quality book. Rule is you edit until you cannot stand to look at the manuscript any more. Then you have it edited by someone else.

This can be a fellow writer, or a professional editor. Family members, unless highly qualified, should not be considered. By that, I mean a family member who is skilled in grammar, punctuation, etc. My sister tears my work apart, sometimes most embarrassingly, but she is excellent, and I do ask her to edit something for me occasionally. I love her dearly, so I don't impose on her too often.

There are two types of editing:

Line editing, where your work is read line-by-line correcting punctuation, grammar, and sentence structure.

Content editing is a little more complicated. Your work is read, line by line, chapter by chapter to look for plot holes, character continuity, correct grammar, writing style, etc.

Using an on-line spell checker is not recommended as the go-to editor.

Your First Five Marketing Strategies

I CALL THEM HOOKS

What is A HOOK?

The HOOK is what you use to HOOK your readers, to HOOK their attention, to hopefully get them interested enough to buy your book. It is your one and only chance to "Make the Sale or Get the Job." If that sounds unusual, it isn't really, it's salesmanship.

You do have several chances to make that first impression, not unlike meeting someone for the first time. It's like a job interview, and in a way, that is exactly what is happening. Someone is interviewing you, (a potential reader), and you hope they will buy your book. (You will get the job)

The first thing they see is your TITLE.

HOOK #1 – TITLE

On Amazon or any book site, the TITLE is your first HOOK. If the Title holds no appeal to the reader, he/she will slide right by yours until he/she finds one that will catch their interest. (These are all Marketing Strategies, by the way.)

The MODERN READER or TODAY'S READER is usually on their mobile device, computer, IPhone, and surfing to find something of interest. Unless they specifically know what it is they are looking for, they are surfing. They are already in their chosen category (Fiction, Non-fiction, Romance. Action/Adventure, etc.) That part is already accomplished.

What does your title say about your book? Does it reflect some sense of the book? Are you completely satisfied with this title? One of the benefits of Self-Publishing, especially on Amazon and KDP (Kindle Direct Publishing), is, you do have the option to make changes. Choose your title carefully so that it reflects what your book is about.

If there is something about the title you aren't comfortable with, then work on making it better. Remember, this is what will attract your reader.

HOOK #2 COVER

Your potential reader likes your title, it's interesting and is a possibility. The next thing your reader looks at is your COVER. Covers that are very busy and have lots of action, illustrations, and printing, do have merits. The reader is going to be looking at a THUMBNAIL, a postage-stamp-size of your cover, so plan accordingly. <u>Sometimes less is better</u>. The key ingredients here are; <u>book title, sub-title (if one) and Author's name</u>. These are what MUST show in the thumbnail of your cover.

There are numerous possibilities for you to consider for your cover. KDP offers the Cover Creator, a program, with which you can DIY a decent cover. I have used CANVA and both programs and had good results. You can also employ the services of a graphic artist who will create the whole thing for you, also which I have done for some of my books.

A web-based program (free) for graphic design is Canva.com.

Here is their link:https://www.canva.com This program is free to use, and they do offer royalty free graphics. You can also purchase graphics for a very nominal fee.

HOOK # 3 YOUR BLURB.

Your BLURB is your introduction or the short paragraph that you will use for the back of your book cover or the paragraph that you will use to best describe what your book is about when you enter this information into the KDP program. This information will be what the public will read when they look at your landing page (the basic page on Amazon that has your cover thumbnail, price, and other pertinent information). KDP has already set up this page for you, free, and this is where your potential reader will be automatically forwarded to when they click on the thumbnail of your cover.

This HOOK #3, Your Blurb, should answer these questions:

WHO

WHAT

WHERE

WHEN

WHY

HOW

The blurb will be like a news story on the front page of a newspaper. It should answer those questions, in fact, that is where those W's came from (journalism).

To break that list down, let's do this:

1. WHO – the who is your main character- who are you writing this book about?
2. WHAT – is happening to this character that the reader should, or might want to identify with, to know more about (the plot).
3. WHERE – where is this taking place? in Chicago, Illinois, along the Amazon River, the Angelic Kingdom? The reader should have some point of reference.
4. WHEN – when is this happening? Years ago, right now, in the future?

5. WHY – what cataclysmic event has happened to the protagonist (hero/heroine) that you have written a story about? Why should the reader read on?

6. HOW - will it be resolved? How will this story end? Make this point like a cliff hanger to make the reader WANT to buy the book. (The Sale, or The Job.).

HOOK #4 FIRST CHAPTER

Amazon KDP offers potential readers a peek (look inside) at the first few chapters of your book, right on your landing page, which gives the reader a better idea of what your book is all about. This is a clever bit of marketing that KDP has already done for you. Your first chapter should also answer those five 'W' questions. Here is where you set up your story (plot) and characters. If they get this far, they are interested, and will probably purchase the book, if not now, then soon. KDP also offers the following, (built right into your landing page)

Read for free – Kindle Unlimited – you still get royalties for this option.

Kindle Matchbook – which ties your print and e-book together.

Buy now with one click – making this easy for the reader.

Deliver to the reader's device (iPhone, tablet, etc.)

Send a free sample

Give as a gift

Add to your list

(this has a pull-down screen with the following):

Kindle Wish List (private)

Shopping list

Kindle Wish List (public)

Gift Ideas List

And finally, if none of the above work, *a Create a List option.*

So, you see, Amazon has done all this marketing for you, and obviously offers all these choices so the reader does not leave your landing page empty-handed. All very clever marketing tools, which benefits both the Author and Amazon.

HOOK #5 AUTHORS' BIO

Reader are curious about who wrote this story. They want to know more about the author, where they come from and what their life is like.

A short bio is all they need to get a glimpse of the author and a peek into her/his personal life. One or two short paragraphs is usually enough to satisfy your reader. One of my students reminded me of this and that is why it is included in the HOOK. It is best to make your bio brief and semi-personal. If you are married and have children, that can be conveyed easily, Have pets? Readers like to know that too.

An easy BIO could read (in third person, please), John is a long time resident of Bath, Maine. He lives with his wife and two young budding writers, a beagle and a cat named Charlie Horse.

There you have it! Brief, personal and cute or intriguing.

A few more words about formatting:

E-Book Formatting

E-books are set up differently from books in print. There is less front matter because the reader is on a device and wants to get to the first chapter, the beginning of the story. Our current readers are SCANNERS rather than studious scholars. They want to read a book quickly (they are most probably reading on the run.) I try to impress that thought upon the members of the writing group.

Your e-book should have the following front matter:

1. Title Page

2. Copyright Page with disclosure and ISBN Number (Optional) Most e-books do not need an ISBN number. This page could also be in the back matter.

3. Dedication page (Optional)

4. Quote if it pertains to the story otherwise "no".

Because your book is on Amazon and they offer that "Look Inside" option, so the sooner your reader gets to your first chapter, the better the chances for the sale.

5. Body of the book

6. Back Matter…

Copyright Page – if you did not place it in the front matter

Acknowledgments

Author's Bio and photo

A list of other books by the author

A thank-you page for buying the book

A list of the author's contact information (website, blog, e-mail address, Goodreads link, Facebook link, Amazon Author Page)

A free first chapter of the sequel (if any)

Print Book Formatting

Your paperback or print book should also have structure, only a lot more and set up differently. Because your first chapter should always start on the right-hand page or an odd numbered page, the pages formatting will look like this.

1. Page one - Title Page

2. Page two - Copyright Page with disclosure and ISBN Number (KDP offers free ISBN numbers). You can use theirs or purchase your own block of ISBN numbers from this site:

http://www.bowker.com/products/ISBN-US.html

Page three - Dedication Page

Page four - Blank

Page five - Acknowledgements page

Page six – blank

Page seven – Quote (optional)

Page eight – Blank

Page nine – Chapter One (odd page)

Body of the book

Blank page at the end of the story or the last chapter. If the chapter ends on an even number page, add another blank page so that your back matter (author's bio) shows on an odd numbered page.

<u>Back Matter</u>:

Author's Bio and photo

    A list of other books by the author

    A thank you page for buying the book

    A list of the author's contact information (web site, blog, e-mail address, Goodreads link, Facebook link, Amazon Author Page)

    A free first chapter of the sequel (if any)

You can see the difference. It is a good idea to go to your library and look at how other print books are set up.

Book Size (Paperback version only)

Many writers with their manuscript clutched in a sweaty hand ready to run, rarely think of what size they should make their book. This is rather important, as it decides what your book will look like when finished.

The default size for KDP Paperback is a 6 x 9 format. My *Blueprinting* Book is written and formatted in a 6 x 9 format, or if I remember correctly, I used the A5 page size which comes close to a 6 x 9. (This was done for you Mac users.)

This *Blue Book* is formatted in 5.25" X 8" because I wanted it to be smaller in size, similar to the *Blue Book Of Cars* salesmen use as a reference.

It is recommended that you go to your library (public or private) and pull out books that look like the size of the book you feel comfortable with.

Bring a small tape measure with you.

Pull out the book and measure it – top to bottom (height) and side to side (width)

This default size is 6 wide and 9 high.

The margins on this Blueprinting are 1" top, bottom, right and left. (one-inch margins all around.)

Margins for a 6 X 9 print book are:

0.75" top

0.75" bottom

0.75" inside

0.5" outside (left margin)

0.13" gutter (the space on the inside of the page to allow for the binding of the book.)

Make certain you click on Mirror Margins so that the pages will work for both pages of your book.

Your Headers and Footers are already at 0.5 so they can stay the same.

There are other variations for this but for our purposes here, let's keep it simple.

What to Do Before You Format

In a separate file that is easily accessible for you, (probably on your desktop) place the following:

1. A perfect author's bio is about two paragraphs long and interesting to read. If you are having difficulties writing your own information, go online and research your favorite authors, read their bios and that should give you some idea of what to say. (NO copying)

2. An up-to-date photo. Important! (The reader wants to see what you look like, not what you used to look like).

3. A list of your personal links to place in the back matter of your book. Include links to your Amazon Author's Page, Face Book page, Website, Blog, Goodread's Author's page and your e-mail address. (it is recommended that you go on the Gmail site and create a new one especially for your books.)

4. Key words and categories for your book when you upload it on KDP.

5. The blurb for the back of your book.

6. You can use this same blurb for your paragraph on your Amazon book page (describing your book).

Put all this information in that file so you have it handy. Believe me, it makes your work a lot easier.

Setting Up Your Accounts

This step is one of the more vital things to carry out so that you can actually publish.

1. This account is where you want your royalties to go, so think about how you want to do this. You will be asked to give your financial information and to fill in tax information for a 1099. Personally, I have a business account with my bank and use this one. You can also use a personal bank account or a savings account. I recommend using an account separate from your personal account.

2. This will also create your book page on KDP where you upload your files to create your actual book.

The screens on KDP will ask you for your title, and so forth down the page until you get to uploading your file and cover. You can stop there.

Let's Talk About Covers

This is important, because, it is your second HOOK!

KDP also offers several cover templates and available options for fonts, colors, and layouts. You can use their free online picture gallery if you wish.

You also have the option of downloading a completely-formatted cover from an outside designer.

Once inside this program, there are further choices to create the perfect cover. I suggest you play with them. The absolute beauty of this program, you can always change anything in your book. Unlike traditional publishing which doesn't allow much in the way of changes.

I have used the KDP program to Create a Paperback and have been satisfied with the results. I use a cover create for my e-book on Canva and modify the back of the cover to fit in one of their templates. When I published my book, *Creating a*

Paperback in KDP, A DIY Guide, proofs were not available nor were author copies. Fortunately, that has changed and you can now order proofs (recommended) and author copies.

A word about Author Copies:

Author copies are a valuable piece in Self-Publishing. These are copies that you can purchase from the printer for a nominal fee.

Example:

Your book is priced at $15.95 retail.

The printing costs are $3.50 per book.

That gives you $12.45 to play with.

You can purchase 10 copies of your book from the printer for $35.00 and sell them at a book signing for the full price, $15.95. You pay the bookstore where you had the book signing either a 30/70 or a 60/40 split or whatever terms you had set. The other option? Offer your book at a discount. Whatever you decide. Fun, isn't it?

Author copies are a valuable marketing tool. Be creative and see how you can use them.

This is what is meant when you have all this control over your books.

If you were with a traditional publisher, your royalties would be much less, and you would get paid quarterly.

Back to covers!

Covers are an expression of what your book is about. It is a peek inside.

You can choose to use a personal photo for your cover but make certain it is yours and you have permissions to use it if there are friends or family portrayed. It is important that you own the rights to that picture or photo.

Another thing to consider is the photo or picture should be in JPEG. format, as that is what KDP will ask for.

Note:

Any pictures and photos should always be in JPG format for printing. Usually digital cameras will save automatically in that format. Also, try to have the picture saved in 300 DPI (Dots Per Inch)

Publishing (finally)

You have your final manuscript ready to go? It is all edited, cleaned up, no spelling errors, etc.

Now save it as (final copy) or some such title so that you always have that final in case you need to go back and make any changes. You can delete all the rest. (they are still safe because they are in your trash) The idea is to get them off your screen or desk-top so you don't become confused.

Now, do two *save as* files. One for KDP as a docx. file, and one *save as* file as a PDF for the cover. Save them to your desk top so that you can find them. Keep that other file folder handy so that you have easy access to your information.

Let's do the e-book first.

Open your book page, and scan down to the '*download your file here*' place. Browse to your docx. file on your desktop, click on it and KDP will download it, change it into their acceptable format

140

and let you know if it worked, usually with a 'download successful' message.

Now move on to download your cover and complete that process.

Follow the prompts until you get to the part where they ask you if you want to preview your book. Follow the prompts and preview your book.

If you need to make changes, you have the final file…

Previewing

Once you have downloaded both your interior and your cover file and the program does it's hurly-gurly processing, you will receive a message asking you if you want to preview your book.

Of course, you do!

Even though you have edited it to almost extinction, do it because sometimes the print formatting does funny things.

<u>Pricing</u>

When you have all the kinks and glitches straightened out, you will move on to another screen where you are asked to price your book. The e-book we already suggested that it be placed between $2.99 to $4.99.

If you go too high, Amazon has a built-in indicator that will give you a price that they have found is based on their past sales and what the market is paying for a book like yours. My suggestion is to go with what they suggest, as they have the stats to back up their suggestion.

Paperbacks are a different story. Your research should have given you an idea of where books like yours are priced. Rule of thumb: page numbers are a direct indicator.

Under 100 pages: up to $9.99

100 to 150 pages - $10.99 to $11.99

160 to 200 pages - $11.99 to $12.99

201 to 250 pages - $12.99 to $13.99

251 to 300 pages - $14.99 to $15.99

And up. These might be a little low, so you might want to check the current market and do your own research. The idea is to sell your book, not to have it commit suicide.

Marketing

The big boo-hoo! Writers and Authors have such a challenging time with this aspect of self-publishing, I am the classic example of "Let me write my books, do I have to market them, too?"

The answer to that is "YES".

What you are reading here is a marketing tool.

Self-publishing is a lot more than just publishing a book. I learned that early. To become successful, you must learn a new set of skills.

The Art of Selling.

Yes, you need to become a salesperson. There are thousands of ideas, methods, and techniques to show you how to do that, and many people who can show you the way. (I am not one of them.)

This is a world I will urge you to explore on your own, HOWEVER, here are some steps you can take to ensure that your book does sell.

I call it, A PLAN FOR EACH BOOK.

A Plan for Each Book

As I was doing my own business plan (Angelic Communications) I wanted to take a good look at each of my books and check them out to analyze why some of them were selling and others were sitting on the screen not doing anything.

Using 3 x 5 cards or a plain sheet, I used one card per book and did a checklist for each one. (Hint: you can also use this form directly on your computer and keep it active in a file somewhere. I recommend a file for each book.)

Also: You can put all this information and your goals up on a calendar. I have post-it notes on the wall above my work station where I can see and reference them.

Here it is:

BOOK: (You fill in the name of your book here.)

_____

CHANGE THIS TITLE?

Does this book need a title change? If it is in print, you can do this by creating a second edition and going through the print process again. If you are publishing digitally, you only need to make those changes in your Microsoft Manuscript saving it as a second edition. If you publish through Amazon.com and their KDP program, you have a dashboard and can make those changes easily, BUT I would wait until I had gone through the entire checklist before dashing off to make any changes there or to any other site.

Another consideration is:

does this title reflect what your book is about?

Example:

Crystal Grids for Light Bodies. The 12 Helixes.

I thought that was a great title, but no one was interested. I had one purchase in several months. My other Crystal Grid books were doing well. I decided to change the title and the cover making it reflect what the book was really about. I changed it

to *Crystal Grids – Activating the 12 Strands of DNA*.
Here are the two covers and the cover changes.

I asked Todd Engel (My cover guru at that time) to make the changes and to simplify the cover.

Another consideration for the best title is to Google it to see if there are other books out there with the same title. Do the same on Amazon under both the print and the e-book section. In another words, do your 'research' or 'homework' again.

COVER

Do you think a new cover will enhance the book? If you made a title change, then you do need a new cover. Not sure? Do some research; check out covers in the same categories and see what is selling and what would easily adapt to your book text. This is like buying and wearing a new outfit.

If you cannot afford a professional designer, you can use www.canva.com or another free or almost-free program. I have used this program for several of my covers and the process is very simple. A key point to remember is - your cover is the first thing a reader sees and uses to push that buy button.

Your cover is the outfit on the model in your store window.

PRICING

Use the same considerations as above. See where the other books in your category are priced. Any shop owner knows that price comparison is a necessary decision. This also implies that you don't have to follow the pack or get into a price war. You want to give your readers honest value for honest monetary compensation.

Unless you are doing a marketing countdown or some sort of offer, personally, I don't recommend selling your book for free unless you have three or four others in a series. Then "free" is your choice. Some authors do this and again, it's their choice.

From a retail standpoint, a shop owner rarely or never offers his merchandise for free. Store owners may offer Marked Down or on Sale, but never for free.

Amazon offers a countdown marketing program for your books, which I have used with some success. They also offer another for a free book but even that has its limitations. I offer my *Funny Bunny* for free during the Easter season, and can offer it for five days. Amazon is a retailer and very savvy in offering merchandise. I have been with Amazon since 2010 and I am pleased with the way they operate and feel that my books have done very well with them.

CATEGORIES

Have you placed your book in the right categories? Sometimes a change here is all that is needed to boost sales. Again, do your research. See what categories other books like yours are in and their ranking. Be honest, make certain you are comparing book content and not what you want yours to be. Ask yourself, is my book really like this one? Should it be in this category? Should you do more research until you are certain this is where your book belongs?

When I went back to review where I had initially placed a few of my older titles, I was appalled. What stretch of my imagination dared me to do that? Also, remember, change! Amazon is adding new categories constantly as demand requires because of their relentless research. As more readers have access to e-books, their searches, and selections change. Remember, not everyone will want to read your books, so your selections here are of the utmost importance. You want to make certain your books are available for your potential readers to find, consider, and purchase.

KEY WORDS

Such an important aspect of what you say about your book. Key words are important and keep your book-up front for the search engines. Yes, we still use those. You can use phrases, and again do your research. Amazon gives you so many choices. Make certain you are in the Kindle e-book section of Amazon if that is where your book is to be presented.

http://keywordtool.io/ is a free online tool that you can use to determine where your book should be and the keywords that are in searches. Your title and your book blurb should have all the keywords you really need and should be the ones prominent in a keyword search.

CONTENT

Does the story or the content need to be re-edited? Many times, after a book is published, the author thinks of changes … we all do it! I have re-published the thinking or thought book four times, each with a different title and upgrading the content.

1. *The 7-Second Thought*
2. *Changing your life with the 7-Second Thought*
3. *Thinking Your Life – The 7-SecondTthought*
4. *What Are You Thinking? Your Thoughts Create Your Life.*

Currently, I am considering another edition for this book, being more specific. The possibilities are endless. I do hope you can see that.

How about the content of your book? The more we write, the better our skills become. Books that you wrote several years ago are probably not the same caliber of writing as your books are now. Check them out to see if I am right!

AUDIO BOOKS

Is this another format you might want to consider? I love audio books and have a very selective library of books from Audible.com on my Smartphone. Audible.com is another Amazon company. Listen to a few or try their introductory free offer and see if you like them. From the first few minutes, I was hooked and could visualize most of my books in audio form. What fun. I have made several attempts at creating one myself and that was even more fun.

TRANSLATION

Can you see this book published in another language? I believe that there are free or almost-free programs to enable a writer to translate their books into other languages. Research is also recommended here.

PUBLISHING E-BOOKS

Here is where you decide if you want to use a service for publishing your books or do it yourself. There are two services that I know of, probably more: **Smash Words** and **Draft2Digital** (D2D). As more and more self-publishers come into this Indie arena, these services will become extremely popular. I am currently using **D2D** and find them tremendously helpful and user friendly. I picture this service much like my personal agent. I give them the book and they send it out to the different sites: Amazon KDP, Kobo, iBook, Nook, Scribed, Inktera, and Tolino. Yes, they do take a small percentage, but you must make that decision, and that is only when the book sells.

I don't want to think of the time it would take me to do all of this individually. Also, just to keep track of this is a nightmare. When would I write?

PRINTED EDITION

This is your decision. If you have a book in your inventory and want to create a print edition, that is up to you. You can do-it-yourself in KDP.

SERIES

If you have written several books in a series, then you might want to consider publishing them as a 'bundle' or offer the first one in the series free so that the rest will automatically be purchased by the reader. This is covered under Marketing Strategies.

FREE SITES

I will list a few sites you can tap into to offer your book for free:

Freebooksy.com

BookGorilla.com,

Booksends.com

There are hundreds more, I am certain, all that is needed is to Google them… I have used Amazon's KDP promotional offers and had a lot of my books downloaded globally. That was fun to watch…

More Marketing Strategies

This area is very important. Writing and Publishing are only half of the story. Here are some of the key ingredients you really should have.

1. **Website** – this is your store front. Amazon does a nice store front on your Author Page.

2. **Blog** – This is your branding – who you are and what you offer.

3. **Podcasts** – More branding, only a little more personal (your voice).

4. **Social Media** - Your audience, and your readers.

5. **Facebook** – Author's Page -- Another store front in another location.

6. **Twitter** – More audience, only a faster pace and condensed version.

7. **Google+** - More audience for branding.

8. **Good Reads** – Another place for branding, except they are already avid readers.

Benefits of Self-Publishing

When you decide to self-publish your manuscript, you have made the decision to have COMPLETE CONTROL of your work. Everything you do with that work, (now and future) is in your hands.

You decide what the book looks like, (the formatting), the cover, and all the physical properties of that work.

You can and should copyright it. (second page after the front cover) Use the copyright symbol (look under insert on your ribbon and search for the symbol ©) Easy. You can follow this up by sending your completed manuscript to the Copyright Bureau. It takes about 16 weeks to receive your confirmation back. Find all that information here:

https://www.copyright.gov/

When you self-publish, you have several options to consider.

1. You can create an e-book.

2. You can create a paperback book.

3. You can create an audio book.

4. You can have the book translated into several languages. German, Mandarin, and Portuguese are the prime languages now.

5. You can create it in a podcast by chapter.

6. You can offer it to magazines as a series.

7. You can create a sequel or series of the book.

I think that gives you an idea of the possibilities one book has.

More Benefits of Self-Publishing

Quote from Wikipedia:

*"**Speed.** An author finds out right away whether a book is a hit with readers; there is not a six-month or longer delay typical with an established publisher since the usual back-and-forth steps with a publisher are bypassed. It is possible to release a book within a few weeks after it's finished.[41] Further, it is possible to avoid the lengthy process of trying to find a literary agent to secure a publishing contract.[71]*

***No start-up costs**. Manuscripts uploaded to KDP or Smashwords typically do not incur any fees.*

***Freedom to begin the next book**. An author can self-publish and then begin work on the next project, potentially being more prolific, although this presumes that the first book won't need any marketing effort.*

A greater share of royalties. Self-published authors earn four to five times more per unit than if an author works with a traditional publisher,[5] sometimes 70% of the sale price.

Pitch books straight to the readers. There is no intermediary censoring what might be shown to the public. The route to readers is more direct."

Another quote from a famous author:

"With self-publishing you don't waste your time trying to get published, which can take years of query letters and agenting, and all this stuff. You go straight to the real gatekeepers, which are the readers. If they respond favorably and you have sales, you can leverage that into a writing career. If they don't, you write the next thing. Either way you're not spending your time trying to get published, you're spending your time writing the next work.

— Hugh Howey, author of Wool

The Good, The Bad and The Ugly

<u>The disadvantages of self-publishing</u>

You might as well have the whole story. (sigh)!!!

Another quote from Wikipedia:

"There are significant challenges to self-publishing as well.

Most self-published books sell few copies. *Some estimates are that they sell fewer than 100 to 150 copies;[7] another estimate is that most sell fewer than 250 copies.[22] However, it should be noted that the vast majority of books promoted by traditional publishers fail as well.[50] Still, the overwhelming odds are that any self-published book will be ignored and end up in the "digital slush pile."[16]*

Authors must spend much time marketing their books. *Authors must work hard to market their* *books, which is a task that many authors are not skilled at or willing to do.[20]*

__Crowded landscape__. There is much competition and it is difficult to get one's book to be noticed in a glutted market.[23] Big publishers have much better prospects for getting attention for a book.[35]

__Lack of prestige__. A book from a traditional publisher still has a lot of cachet in that it has been vetted by editors, which gives it a "stamp of approval."[71][2]

__Hard to get into bookstores__. Big bookstores rarely take self-published books, and if they do, they want 50% of the sales price.[2] Publishers have established distribution channels to make this easy.

__Difficulty getting reviews in the mainstream press__. It is difficult for self-published books to be reviewed in newspapers and magazines. The media favors books from traditional publishers before giving reviews.[2][98]

Having to spend time marketing the book. One self-published author in Britain was working "14 hour days", spending months promoting her book *Only the Innocent*; while she eventually made it to the UK Kindle bestseller chart, Rachel Abbott still has difficulty getting the publishing world to take her book seriously.[99] Another writer, Ros Barber, thinks self-publishing is a "terrible idea for serious novelists" since the requirements of marketing and promoting a book will prevent one from writing, and he continues to recommend the traditional approach.[98]

Self-published books usually ineligible for prizes. Books are not eligible for major prizes such as the Hay festival, the Booker, the Baileys, the Costa and the Man Booker, and literary novels need these prizes to become a bestseller.[98] However, there are signs that this is changing as more books become self-published."

Now that I have given you the dark side of self-publishing, here are some statistics that you may want to look at before you make the final decision to self-publish or not.

The Author Earnings Report. This report is published every two years. We shall see an up-to-date one soon.

https://thenewpublishingstandard.com/tag/author-earnings-report-2018/

Congratulations! I wish you Happy Writing and Happy Self-Publishing.

Cheers!

Sharon

Before We Say Adieu…

I would love to help you get that first book formatted and published. Once you learn how to do it, the second and successive books are easier.

I am creating several detailed step-by-step courses to help writers who are serious about starting this new career.

If you feel that this would be of interest, please sign up below to become a member of the Cape Cod Writers' Studio.

Here is my contact information if you need to speak with me directly:

audacious-publisher@gmail.com

My website:

www.audacious-publisher.com

My blog: (you can also access this through my web site)

www.audacious-author.com

There, I've said it all!

Remember to check out the Cape Cod Writers' Studio and their website: (Hint: I'm still building it.)

www.capecodwritersstudio.com

Happy writing and publishing!

Sharon D. Anderson

Cape Cod, Massachusetts

May 2019

Thank you

for buying my book. I appreciate your consideration and hope that it has been helpful to you in your self-publishing career.

Could you please leave a brief review on the site where you purchased this book? Reviews help other writers decide if the information is helpful.

Huge Hugs

Sharon

AVAILABLE AS E-BOOK FORMAT

AVAILABLE IN PRINT ** starred title

ALL BOOKS CAN BE FOUND ON-LINE

Visionary Fiction

Atlantis – The Final Days**

Angels in Action

All Cooped Up**

A Cape Cod Romance

A Christmas Wish**

Dear Angels**

Stones and Bones**

The Something Series

Something Witchy the pilot**

Something Witchy – Book one**

Something Sinister - Book two**

Something Bloody - Book three **

Something Loverly - Book four**

Something Merry – Book five **

Visionary Non-Fiction

Creating Crystal Grids**

Sacred Grids**

Crystal Grids for Light Bodies

Crystal Grids for Personal Protection**

What Are You Thinking? **

Cosmic Blueprint**

Raising Your Energy**

Body Blogs for Health**

Children's Book

Tuk-Tuk the Rabbit**

The Black Shadow**

Spiritual Guidelines Series

Now a Boxed Set*

Prosperity Workbook

Remarkable Relationships

To Your Health**

Everyone is Evolving

ON WRITING

Writing as a Retail Business**

Creating a Paperback in KDP**

Blueprinting for Successful Self-Publishing**

The Blue Book of Self-Publishing**

Sharon D. Anderson, PhD, RMT

Sharon is an Author/Publisher, dedicated to writing Heavenly Cozy Mysteries. Founder of the Cape Cod Writer's Studio which meets weekly in Dennis Port, Centerville and Cotuit, she helps the members self-publish their work, supporting them on their paths to publication with many pots of tea and lots of biscuits…

She is a member of Visionary Fiction Alliance, and Cape Cod Writer's Center.

Her website:

https://www.audacious-publisher.com

E-mail: sdanderson.books@gmail.com

Her Blog/website:

https://www.audacious-author.com